Ex Libris

SCHULZ

© UNITED FEATURE SYNDICATE, INC.

A FARM

Carl Larsson

With paintings by Carl Larsson
and a text by Lennart Rudström
based on the artist's original text

Translated by Ernest Edwin Ryden

First American Edition 1976. Illustrations copyright © 1966
by Albert Bonniers Förlag AB. English text copyright ©
1976 by G. P. Putnam's Sons. All rights reserved. Published
simultaneously in Canada by Longman Canada Limited,
Toronto. SBN: GB-399-61031-6 SBN: TR-399-20541-1
Library of Congress Catalog Card Number: 76-2130
Printed in Portugal 1976, by Gris Impressores

G. P. Putnam's Sons   New York

What a wonderful thing it must be for an artist who paints landscapes to have his own farm and a horse and pigs and chickens. That's what Carl Larsson thought. Still, he did own Little Hyttnäs (The Hut-on-a-Point), a cottage in Sundborn, in the province of Dalarna. That's where he liked to be in the summer—painting in the country. When autumn came and it was dismal, he took his family back to Stockholm.

One day as he sat at home in town with the wind blowing and the rain drumming on the window-panes, a letter arrived from Björk at the farm Spadarvet, next door to Little Hyttnäs. Björk wrote that the property was for sale with four cows, one horse, one pig, some sheep—and chickens, of course.

In early spring when the snow melted and ran from the rooftops and gutters, Carl Larsson took his wife and children to Sundborn to buy Spadarvet. On March 10, 1897, his dream of owning a farm came true.

But since he wanted to continue to paint, he needed someone to look after the farm. That's how Johan and his wife, Johanna, and Tekla and Bäckström came to be hired.

Carl Larsson rebuilt the old houses on the farm, and he built some new ones. Next door at his painter's cottage, Little Hyttnäs, he added a large room where he could paint and where the family could celebrate birthdays and name days and Christmas Eve.

One day as the artist was painting out on the hill, along came Johanna with Blossom, the cow. *Now that is a lovely scene,* thought Carl Larsson. *I will paint the two of them.*

And I will paint the whole farm, everything there is to see. I will paint Johan and Bäckström as they work in the forest. I will paint when we sow and harvest, and when we pick apples in the fall, and when we plow and harrow, and when we dig ditches in the spring.

And Christmas at the Larssons', the lovely Christmas in the big parlor. Yes, I will paint that, too....

Carl Larsson was born in the "old city" of Stockholm. He wrote that if he had been born in the country, he would undoubtedly have become a farmer. Instead, he became an artist—an artist who wanted to own a farm. With the money he received for his great wall painting in the National Museum, he was able to buy Spadarvet.

Johan and Johanna, who ran it, lived on the farm, while Carl Larsson, his wife, Karin, and all their children continued to live at Little Hyttnäs next door.

The youngest child was called Esbjörn. He is to be found in many of the paintings here.

New Year's had just come and gone, and the Christmas festivities for the year were over. Now it was time to get back to work, and Johan and Bäckström were going into the woods with their tools.

They took a saw, an ax, and a wedge. And a coffeepot, for it had turned bitterly cold and the coffee would help keep them warm. The temperature had dropped to twenty degrees, and icicles formed in their nostrils when they drew in their breaths. When they exhaled the air, it looked just like a chimney!

As soon as they arrived at the clearing in the woods, they started a fire and set up the coffeepot. Then they warmed their hands over the fire, for they were chilled through and through. Bäckström was so cold that he moved about slapping his arms while he waited for the coffee to heat up.

"It's sad to see the forest clearings around here getting sparse," Johan said.

But the cows needed a place to graze in summer, so they had to clear away some of the woods.

Johan felled the trees with his saw, and Bäckström trimmed them with his ax. Then Johan lifted the logs to the sawbuck and divided them into lengths of one meter each. The saw had just been filed, and its teeth adjusted, so it was a pleasure to use.

Bäckström split the toughest sections with his ax and wedge. When he had a good-sized pile, he straightened up and gazed beyond the treetops. He wanted to check the wind and weather. Then he began to stack the logs in neat piles. He always took care that the bark was on the upper side, so that the logs wouldn't get soaked when it rained.

When he had cut and stacked a good pile of wood, Bäckström added more logs to their fire and poured himself another cup of coffee. Johan too filled his mug with the steaming drink. There they sat, Johan and Bäckström, feeling the warm glow of the fire and listening to the wind sigh through the branches of the tall fir trees.

After a little while Johan said to Bäckström, "Let's get back to work now. Evening is coming on."

The woods that were part of the farm were not large, nor were they thick. They could be used only for some firewood. *If only there were better forests here,* thought Carl Larsson, *then we could use the lumber for building houses.*

In those days it was hard work laboring in the forests, as you can see in this nineteenth-century illustration. There were no power saws, and one had to work with a simple handsaw, both in felling trees and in cutting them into lumber. It was important that one's saw was newly filed and that its teeth were properly adjusted. Tongs were used to bend every other tooth to the right or to the left. This prevented the saw from sticking in the moist wood.

It was also time to get busy with the storing of ice. It had to be cut and put away before the end of February. In the warmer months the ice would get wet and porous. It should be fine and solid, and as hard and clear as glass, for the harder the ice, the longer it would last.

One afternoon, when Bäckström and Johan had finished cutting wood in the forest clearing, Johan said, "Tomorrow, Bäckström, we will put up the ice."

So on the following day they hitched Brunte to the bobsleigh and drove down to Lake Toftan. They had loaded the sleigh with the big ice saws and boat hooks, and they wore heavy overcoats, for it would certainly be cold out on the ice. The coffeepot was brought along, too. In this weather it went with them everywhere. They stopped by the church, unhitched Brunte, and gave him a bag of hay. Brunte stood munching while Johan and Bäckström began to saw the ice.

The big saws made muffled sounds as they went up and down through the thick ice. The water bubbled and splashed around their feet.

"It is good and solid," remarked Bäckström.

Johan agreed. Last year's ice had been far inferior to this.

When there were a large number of ice cakes splashing around in the water, Johan fetched Brunte and fastened the hooks under the first cake of ice to be raised. Then they smacked the horse's flanks, and Brunte gave a mighty pull. The ice cake almost flew out of the water. It glittered and glowed brightly in the sun. One cake after another was brought ashore.

Then they put pine branches around the open places where they had removed the ice. They were careful about this. Otherwise, someone might come along and stumble in.

Just before twilight, they drove home to place the ice in storage, covering it with sawdust to keep it frozen until summer.

In those days people did not have the facilities for freezing and preserving food as we have today. Instead, they gathered ice from the lakes in the winter to have it for summer.

If one could get the clear core ice, it would keep better. The ice saws were more than six feet long, and they had sawteeth about two and one-half inches in size. The ice storage shed was near the farm. Once the ice was stored, a layer of fine, dry sawdust about twenty inches thick was used to cover it. If it were done properly, it would preserve the ice through the summer and even into the late fall. One could then go and chop a piece of ice as needed or place food to be preserved with the stored ice.

A lot of work had to be done on the farm before spring arrived. It was not only clearing in the woods, storing the ice, and caring for the animals, but also checking to see what needed to be repaired or replaced. Sometimes sleighs and sleds had to be built. Often shafts for the sleighs needed replacing. Shafts were the long pieces of wood between which the horses were hitched to a sleigh.

Whenever the weather was bad, Johan could be found in the carpenter's shed, making new shafts for Brunte and Lisa or perhaps building a sleigh. He carved beautiful figures on the sleighs he built.

Johan always whistled a tune while he worked in the shed, for he liked to be there. He had all the tools he needed: axes and saws, planes and chisels and drills. He also had a fine, sharp knife for carving. That was what little Esbjörn liked to look at the most.

And here also was the pleasant smell of various kinds of trees: birch and fir and juniper. Occasionally Johan would bend over and pick up a bit of shaving and smell it. He liked its pleasant odor. Esbjörn did, too.

"Will you fix my spade, Johan?" Esbjörn asked.

Johan was happy to repair it, for Esbjörn was his friend and he had given him the spade. Johan lit the flame under the glue pot. He glued the spade and placed it in a vise. Then he smoothed out all the rough spots.

Esbjörn stayed with Johan all day long and helped him as best he could. After several hours, twilight set in, and Johan lit the kerosene lamp. He told Esbjörn that it was getting dark and it would soon be time to go home for their evening meal. They would continue their work the next day.

Esbjörn agreed. He was hungry, and besides, he almost always agreed with Uncle Johan.

Every farm had a carpenter's cabin and sometimes a little forge. In the forge they repaired wagon wheels and forged axes, sledgehammers, and spades. They also made tools and utensils, such as chisels, planes, and hammers.

In the carpenter's shed they made new furniture and wooden implements that were used for cultivating the land. Everything was made by hand, for they had no machinery. They sawed and bored and planed and sanded—all by hand. It was slow work, but it was important that things were made strong and would last for many years. Here in the province of Dalarna there was a lot of birch, and it was often used in woodwork.

Hay rakes were always of wood, and every prong was cut with a knife. The shop stayed filled with hay rakes with broken prongs to be repaired.

Every morning during April Johan rowed over to Bullerholm Bay to examine the bow net and other nets. Sometimes the sun shone, and sometimes it was misty. But often a chilling spring rain was falling. The water was cold, and one's fingers got completely numb in the icy slush. Even one's fingernails ached.

But there were plenty of fish. Johan even caught pike, a favorite. They were not large—perhaps five or six inches long. But they were fine for eating.

Perch and fat pickerel were also plentiful. But the pickerel had lots of bones. Eating one was almost like putting a packet of sewing needles in one's mouth.

Fishing here on a windy spring day was not easy. Johan had to keep the boat steady even in the harshest wind. Just as he caught a fine pike, a sudden gust of wind might make Johan lose the pike and the net, and the boat would go flying clear across the bay and into the birch grove with its overhanging branches and brushwood. The water was high everywhere, for the snow was melting.

After Johan had inspected the nets, he rowed home with slow, deliberate strokes. And he thought to himself, *When I get home, how glad they will be to see the fine pike.* But he also reminded himself that he would soon have to make some new nets. *The old ones I have made are getting rather worn*, he thought. *Next spring I'm going to have some fine new nets to set in Bullerholm Bay.*

In those days a Swedish farmer had to do almost everything himself. Not only did he have to be a blacksmith and a carpenter, but he also had to take care of all the fishing equipment, not only repairing the nets, but making new ones.

Here Johan is shown inspecting a net. He must lift it out of the water, remove the fish, and then let it sink back to lie in the same place. Johan is about to remove a pike. He has already taken the perch from the net.

Nearly opposite Johan lies the bow net, which he will inspect as soon as he is through with the large net. A bow net was like a long sack which a fish could easily enter but had great difficulty finding a way out of. Bow nets were usually left lying in places where the fish are known to swim in the spring.

The birch leaves had just come out and were no larger than mouse ears. But the birds were already singing their spring songs. On this morning, when Johan went out on the hill, he could tell by the air that the time to harrow the fields had come. Harrowing would break up the ground that had been frozen all winter to get it ready for planting.

He went in to find Bäckström, who was eating his breakfast to tell him that they could get busy with the spring sowing.

"We are having fine weather, Bäckström. We had better get started today," he said.

So they went out to the barn on the hill and hitched up the horses to the harrows—Brunte to the heavier spring-tooth harrow and Lisa to the lighter one.

The field they were to harrow had been grassland for a number of years. But the autumn before they had plowed it up, and today Johan would sow it with oats. The harrow went in all directions. Dust rose in clouds from the dry ground. Lumps of earth were broken, and tufts of grass went flying into the air.

Spring had truly come, and it was as warm as a summer's day.

Johan's and Bäckström's faces were almost black from dust and perspiration.

"It is seventy degrees in the sun," Bäckström said.

It certainly was hot. Even the horses were beginning to perspire. Tekla went around kicking to pieces some of the stubborn lumps of earth. She was tired and hot and irritable from the hard work.

"In just one day the birches have already turned darker in color," Johan said to Bäckström. "We had better hurry now and sow the oats. We should do it before the day is over."

As they headed toward home with the horses, they could see the crows and sea gulls invading the field. They were strutting about, picking up the finest dew worms they could find.

Timothy grass had been growing in this field. But in the autumn it was plowed under, and the ground was allowed to lie fallow over the winter. Nothing was planted, to give the soil a chance to rest.

But now it was spring and time for sowing. First the ground must be harrowed thoroughly. The harrow must be drawn over it three or four times. The feather harrow that Brunte is pulling is new and certainly much better than the claw harrow that people had used in earlier days. Tekla's job, which was common, belonged to an earlier period. It was called lump breaking and was hard work. But the earth had to be loose and fine. Many years passed before the first tractors capable of pulling heavy rollers were built. Then people no longer had to break up the lumps in the fields by hand.

The end of that day was slow in coming. Johan and Bäckström and Tekla and all the others had eaten their supper early, and the horses had been given water and hay. Then they went back to work and continued long into the twilight.

Oats had to be sown. Bäckström hitched Brunte to the light harrow and drove out to the field ahead of the others.

Johan hitched the mare, Lisa, to the open-sided wagon, and brought sacks of seed to the birch grove. He hurried home with the horse and cart before he began to sow.

It is like the loveliest evening in summer, thought Johan, *and it is only May.*

Tekla helped keep Johan supplied with oats. Johan used both hands when he sowed, first to the right, then to the left, then right again, and then to the left. The seed flew out in big circles and lay in patterns when it hit the ground. The last rays of the sun burned Johan's neck as it began to set behind the ridge.

Each time Johan went down the hill he could see his long blue shadow go ahead of him. It became longer and longer every time he turned.

When the sun finally went down, it began to get dark quickly, and Johan told Bäckström and Tekla, "That's enough for today."

But Bäckström wanted to finish what remained to be done.

"I can harrow just as well when it gets as dark," he said. "And the oats must get into the ground."

In those days there were no machines for sowing seed. One had to sow by hand, and that took a lot of time. Nor could one be careless. It was important for the seed to fall smoothly and evenly on the ground, so that it would come up smooth and close. Not everybody was allowed to sow. Usually it was the farmer himself who did it. Here Johan is sowing the oats. By fall they should be ready to harvest.

As soon as the seed was sown, it had to be harrowed into the ground. Otherwise, there was the risk that it might dry out or that the birds might come and eat it up.

In those days one harrowed lightly after the seed had been sown. Nowadays, however, the planting machine buries the seed at the proper depth.

The first real summer rain arrived, and the fields, the meadows, and the woods smelled fragrant and sweet. Larger leaves appeared on the birches, the first swallows arrived, and wood anemones began to bloom in the pasture.

Johanna told Johan that she thought it was time to put the cows out to pasture.

The next morning Johan went to the cowshed and turned Blossom and Dolly and the other cows loose to roam on the farm's hillside. They jumped and leaped and kicked and butted one another playfully. They held their tails straight up in the air and bellowed.

The following morning Lill-Tekla and little Kersti went down to the farmyard and called to the cows. They were finally going to be sent out to pasture in the woods. Lill-Tekla led the way. She sang and called. First came the bell cow, Blossom, and then Dolly and Kajsa and Fina and Krona and Krusa. Little Kersti came along behind and urged them on with catkins, for they stopped everywhere to snatch bits of grass.

The sheep were already in the parsonage pasture, and as soon as they saw the cows, they began to bleat and run away. The cows bellowed worse than ever. But soon they were grazing on grass and leaves.

The girls would stay here and watch the cows all day. Where the sun shone through the branches, it was warm and dry. Since Lill-Tekla was barefoot, she stood in a sunny place where the warmth felt good on her feet. She was working on a ribbon that she wanted to finish by evening. When her feet got chilly, she moved to another sunny spot.

Little Kersti sat on a rock and petted Krusa as she nosed after the salt that Kersti had in her apron pocket. The flies buzzed, and yellow butterflies fluttered around the landscape. The cows mooed, and the sheep answered from the parsonage pasture.

Summer had come.

May was the time to turn the animals out to pasture. It was always a spirited dance. The cows went berserk. They turned their tails straight up into the air and leaped and bounded about wildly. As for the calves, who found themselves outdoors for the first time, they carried on even worse. The shepherd girl had to keep a close eye on them so they wouldn't harm themselves. Sometimes she had to entice the cows with both salt and hominy she carried in her apron pocket. Here in the picture they have already arrived in the pasture. The shepherdess is standing and weaving on a ribbon loom that she has brought with her. The days could get so long out here in the woods, and the loom was so light and fine it could be carried anywhere. It helped pass the time.

The shepherd girls and boys always occupied themselves with some kind of work when out in the woods.

In the early evening all the cows and sheep were taken home again.

"Come, cows. Come now," Tekla cried. The bell cow, Blossom, led the way. The whole long row of cows followed her, bellowing, for they wanted to get home to be milked.

The sheep went into their pens, and the cows into their stalls. Later, when Johanna came into the barn, the cows stood and stared at her, mooing as though they were greeting her.

Johanna took down the milk stool and the clean, shining milk pan and went to Krusa, who stood nearest her and was a fine milk cow. Johanna patted Krusa and moved her a bit so she could place the milk pan under her. Then she wiped the nipples, greased them with a little fat, and began to milk.

While she sat there, she prattled to the cows all the time. If Krusa did not stand still, Johanna muttered to her. And if one of the cows accidentally kicked over the milk pan and sent the milk spilling everywhere, Johanna really got mad.

"Stand still!" she shouted so loudly that the cat, who was lying there asleep, looked around in fright, wondering what was going on. But soon Johanna forgot she was angry and gave the cat a squirt of milk on a saucer that always stood in a corner. Then she went on milking as though nothing had happened.

Before Johanna left for the night, she cleaned the stalls and spread straw on the floor, pumped water into the trough, and gave the sheep hay and grain.

"Good night to you and sleep well," she always said when she closed the door to the barn. But the cows never answered her. All she heard was the contented sounds of munching and chewing.

Here Johanna is sitting and milking with her hands. There were no machines, and Johanna had to milk in a large bucket. The only machine in the picture is the large red water pump. For that time it was considered very modern and convenient to get water from a pump without carrying it in buckets from the well.

The cows weren't always brought into the barn to be milked. Sometimes they were milked out on the hill and then let loose to return to the woods to stay overnight.

The stalls were cleared of manure with a large manure fork. Then they were swept clean with a birch broom, and peat and straw were spread in the barn and stalls. When the cows were kept indoors, this had to be done both morning and evening.

It was the first week in July, and Johan wanted to start the mowing.

The mowing machine was new, and Brunte had not yet become used to the noisy, clattering contraption. Still, he pulled it steadily, even though he laid his ears back from time to time and looked questioningly at Johan, who sat there bobbing up and down on his seat.

Everything fell before the blade of the mowing machine: timothy grass, oxeye daisies, buttercups, and bluebells.

Bäckström operated the drag rake, while Johanna and Tekla raked after him.

The rye was fine. *Rasp, rasp* went the scythe as it swung back and forth. Johan perspired in the midsummer heat. But when the sun disappeared behind storm clouds on the horizon, Johan worried. It must not rain now in the middle of the rye harvest. Johanna and Tekla walked immediately behind Johan and bound the sheaves. "They are fine ears this year," Johanna said.

But why didn't Tilda come with the four o'clock coffee? Had she forgotten them? No. There she was coming along with a basket dangling from her arm.

While Johan and Johanna, Tekla and Bäckström drank coffee, Tilda picked the bluebells that grew in the midst of the rye.

Later in the autumn the threshing machine was brought into the barn. Brunte was hitched to it just outside the barn door, and he went there around and around in a ring, pulling to make it operate. The machine rumbled and roared: *to-ka-dee, to-ka-dee, to-ka-dee.* Tekla collected the sheaves and threw them to Johan, who fed them into the machine. Johanna raked away the chaff, and Bäckström gathered it together on a hay fork and threw it up to the boys in the hayloft. After the threshing came the winnowing. They had to get rid of the chaff so that only the seed grain remained.

Bäckström operated the winnowing machine, and Johan fed it with grain. The heavy grain seeds fell near the machine, while the lighter chaff floated down near the wall. Then the hens came, the rooster in the lead. The rooster crowed with delight, declaring that he was the greatest rooster in the world. But Johan chased them all away. No roosters or hens were allowed to peck at this seed.

Here, in the province of Dalarna, harvesting began the first week in July. Farther south in Sweden it started around midsummer.

The mowing machine was a new agricultural tool. In former days the grain was cut with a scythe. Now it was no longer necessary to call on friends and neighbors to help gather the harvest. Only the rye still had to be cut with a scythe. It would be some time before the first harvesting machine capable of both cutting the grain and binding it into sheaves would be invented.

Here the women are binding the sheaves by hand. A threshing machine in the barn, with a horse outside serving as a "motor," was considered very modern, as was that beautiful blue winnowing machine. With this new invention it was no longer necessary to thrash the grain with a flail or to stand and fling the grain across the inside of the barn to separate the seed from the chaff.

When Johan and Bäckström opened the church door, they heard the congregation already singing the second stanza of the first hymn:

> The falling raindrops praise Thee,
>   And e'en the gentle breeze;
> Angelic choirs adore Thee,
>   And fall upon their knees.
> And lo! the mighty ocean
>   And flowing brooks ashore
> Declare Thy love and goodness,
>   Our God forevermore.

Johan and Bäckström were late this day because one of the cows had given birth to a calf that morning. The church bells had already started ringing eleven o'clock when they finally got started.

Instead of sitting in their usual places, they sat a little farther back in the church. When the hymn came to a close, the pastor turned toward the altar to pray.

Johan sat and gazed around. He recognized every neck in Sundborn. Directly in front of him sat little Esbjörn. He was not very tall, and his head just reached to the top of the pew.

From time to time Johan looked at Esbjörn. The small boy gazed at the paintings above the altar: the two angels with the white wings and the dove between them that seemed to be flying right into the church and the two chandeliers of brass that hung from the ceiling, gleaming in the sun. Now and then Esbjörn looked in the hymnbook. He discovered that someone had turned the corner of one of the pages, and Esbjörn turned it back again.

But when the pastor had preached in the pulpit a long time, Esbjörn got tired, and he had a hard time staying awake. He nodded and drifted off to sleep. Johan and Bäckström smiled.

In the old-time churches in the agricultural areas, the various farms had their individual pews. And there they sat at worship, the women on one side of the center aisle and the men on the other. And undoubtedly it happened that someone who had worked hard all week was so tired that he fell asleep, just like little Esbjörn. The man in the fine blue cape was the church caretaker, but in earlier days he was known as the church thumper. It was his business to go around and arouse those who had a hard time keeping awake. In this illustration, however, he is holding the offering bag.

Far to the front is the pastor, robed in red altar vestments.

Today organs are found in almost every church, but then a cantor stood in the chancel to lead the singing. Carl Larsson painted the angels and the dove above the altar.

The hens thrived almost as well on the manure pile as they had inside the barn in the midst of the newly threshed grain, where they were not allowed. The rooster was even more cocky here, where he felt more at home. Usually he could be found standing on one leg, cocking his head, and crowing as loudly as possible.

Now there was going to be a more permanent enclosed manure shelter where the sun and wind could not dry out the fine, fine fertilizer.

When Elfström came and began to saw and hammer, the rooster was furious and crowed worse than ever.

"Oh, yes," Elfström muttered. "You have the whole hill to yourself. You certainly don't need to crow yourself to death just because I am standing here sawing."

Elfström had finished setting up all the posts and covered half the walls with boards before the rooster would move.

And then he went here and there, fussing about. He didn't calm down until Elfström had finished and he saw that an opening had been left where he could stroll in and out of the manure pile just as he pleased.

"There you see, you silly rooster," Elfström said, "you didn't have to fuss so much about nothing."

Bäckström had begun to load the decomposed manure into the cart. It had to be brought out to the fields. Lisa, the mare, did not want to stand still today, and after a few flings with the pitchfork, Bäckström had to get out and back her up a bit. But Bäckström was in a good mood today, so he didn't complain. There was a lot going on this day. Everybody in the village was invited to Johan's house for coffee at two o'clock. It was Johanna's birthday, and everyone had hoisted a flag in celebration.

A large amount of manure accumulated during the winter in the barn, the stalls, and the pigpens. All this was deposited in the dung yard and left to lie and "burn," as it was called. To burn meant that it was left on the ground, drawing its powerful acids out. Otherwise, there was danger that the crops might be burned instead.

But even if the manure had to be burned, there was the danger that it might be exposed to excessive sunlight or too much rain. Then it became too weak to be a good fertilizer. That is why they built an enclosure of boards to contain it. They spread a bit of straw or earth or peat moss over the heap to keep it from sending forth such a strong odor.

Formerly oats and timothy had grown in this field, but the earth had been left fallow for an entire year to rest.

During the winter Johan and Bäckström had carted manure to the field. They had placed the manure in piles and had covered the piles with earth, which they had stamped down flat.

Now Johan and Bäckström spread the piles of manure over the field before going to dig up the potatoes in another field. They were already a few days late getting to the potatoes.

Johan filled the cart, throwing big pitchfork loads into it, to make it easier to spread the piles evenly over the field. Johan was strong—stronger than most of the men in the village. He was able to work long into the night if necessary.

It was important to get the fertilizer spread as soon as possible; otherwise, it might spoil. Johan planned to harrow it into the soil on the morrow.

A fresh northern breeze was blowing, and it was much colder than usual. Brunte's mane fluttered in the wind. This was not the most pleasant kind of work for a horse. Not even a blade of grass at the edge of the ditch. And Johan now was in a hurry. They must just continue to work and work.

Rye would be grown here. Before the first snow, tender rye shoots would appear above the ground. It would not be ready to harvest until the next autumn. Then Johan and Johanna and Tekla and Tilda and Bäckström would be found here hard at work.

And Brunte and Lisa would bring home the sheaves to the barn and the thresher.

Johan spread the manure with the help of a horse and cart and pitchfork. At New Year's time he had put piles of manure in the field, and these piles now made good fertilizer. It was not his favorite kind of work. It was heavy and dirty. At this time only natural manure was used. Artificial fertilizer had not been developed. Eventually the mechanical spreader came into use, and then the work was easier. After that, one needed only to load the fertilizer into the spreader, drive onto the field, and let the horse go. The spreader did the rest, throwing the fertilizer evenly on the ground. Certainly it was a great forward step.

Here the manure had to be harrowed immediately into the ground to keep it from drying out.

"Tomorrow we will dig the potatoes," Johan announced. But Bäckström could not join them. He had his own potato field to dig. Little Esbjörn was to work in Bäckström's place.

Johan had dug up a few potatoes to examine them. He peeled them, and they looked ready for digging. He told the children, "Now, children, we must arrange for a potato holiday from school. We will dig the potatoes on the Kart hill tomorrow."

Johan began by cutting off the tops of the potato plants and drying them. Then he hitched Brunte to the work surrey, loaded it with the women and children, a wooden plow, baskets and buckets, and drove up to the Kart hill.

The Kart hill was a good place for potatoes, and it looked as if it were going to be a fine potato year.

Johan and Brunte plowed one furrow after another. The potatoes gleamed like lumps of gold in the black soil. The children competed with each other. They filled buckets and boxes and baskets. But Esbjörn, that sly little boy, skipped all the small potatoes. Only giant-sized potatoes were found in his bucket. And they all were fine and clean, for he had rubbed off all the dirt with his thumb. Every time his bucket was full he ran around and showed it to Johan and Tekla and Tilda and all the other children. But in places where Esbjörn had picked, Johanna had to take an extra turn. She said nothing, picking as before. She knew that Esbjörn picked only the largest potatoes.

After four days all the potatoes were picked. Johan drove home with the sacks to be placed in the potato cellar. Everyone was paid according to what he or she had picked, and each one was given a sack of potatoes as well. Esbjörn received five shillings in wages.

Then the heavy rains came and continued for several days. Esbjörn told everyone that it certainly was fortunate that he had helped, or who knows how things might have turned out?

When the potatoes were ready to be dug up in September, it was important to have lots of help from both children and adults. They had to take advantage of days when the weather was fine because if the potato fields were wet and muddy, the work would take twice the time.

A horse and wooden plow were used to raise the earth so the potatoes were exposed. It was important to pick fast. A hand hoe was helpful, for there were usually potatoes hidden in the ground. This illustration shows fourteen people working in the field. Children were excused from school to help.

Today a mechanical potato digger is attached behind a tractor, but people are still needed to hand-pick and sort the potatoes.

It now was late in fall and time for fall plowing. Bäckström took hold of the plow handles, set the plowshare into the oatfield, arranged the reins, and gave Brunte a smack. Brunte struggled forward and pulled. Soon the stubble field disappeared, and the earth came forth dark and shining. Steam came from Brunte's nostrils, revealing how cold it already was.

More and more birch leaves floated to the ground. Every morning there was fog. And rain, and wind, and storm. And it blew just like a hurricane—almost, Esbjörn said.

Johan and Bäckström dug ditches as fast as they could.

They stood with their backs bent over almost all day. Once in a while they straightened up, and when the rain became too heavy, they went home to rest near the cookstove and warm themselves.

Snow fell early this year. When it did, Bäckström hitched Lisa to the sleigh and drove out to the charcoal kiln in the forest. Engström lived there in a charcoal cabin. He was a charcoal maker through and through, and his whole face was black from the charcoal. Engström loved to sing. In the evenings he lay in his cabin alone and sang ballads. Anyone passing by in the evenings could hear him.

For several weeks Bäckström and Engström made charcoal for the farm. The charcoal kiln had to be operated carefully. When they had put out the fire in the kiln and removed the blower, Bäckström returned to the farm. He was covered in coal dust when he came home, and everyone laughed at him. But he didn't mind. To live in the charcoal cabin a few weeks in the fall was one of the most enjoyable experiences he could imagine.

Soon it was the first week in December. Now everyone got busy. There was scouring and baking and decorating to be done. And the pig had to be slaughtered. The butcher came and did that.

They made Christmas ham and Christmas sausage and preserves. They made so much of everything that there was plenty for all who had worked on the farm during the year.

"Welcome, everybody, for Christmas Eve! And, Johan, don't forget your violin!" Carl Larsson said, when he invited them all to come to Little Hyttnäs to celebrate.

Once the harvest was done, plowing took up the most time. Plowing can also be done in the spring, but it isn't as good a time.

Digging ditches by hand was a lot of work, too. Today tile pipe is laid in the ditch and covered with earth so that it is possible to drive with tractors and reapers between fields and meadows.

Charcoal furnaces are no longer found. In the illustration one can see how they made charcoal to supply the big blast furnaces, in which iron was melted. Today coal is used, or the iron is melted in large electric furnaces.

They slaughtered for Christmas in December. It must not be done too close to Christmas, however, for there would not be time enough to make the sausage and cooked ham and preserves.

Finally, it was Christmas Eve in the big living room at the Larssons'. All the guests had arrived. There were Johan and Johanna and Sanna. Johan had brought his violin under his arm. Bäckström and his wife were there. The old grandfather was given the big chair. The aged Holm looked in for a while. The girls in the kitchen came in. Susanne and Lisbeth passed the bread. And Karin said, "Step up now and have a taste of everything: the ham and sausage and meat balls and meat loaf."

Little Esbjörn had already tasted the meat balls. Only a little bit, just the edge of one of them, and even then he had put it back. Oh, yes, even the cat had received a little taste.

Everyone ate as much as he could. And since it was Christmas Eve, they all helped themselves several times. Coffee was served, with saffron buns, cookies, and cream puffs.

When they were finished, Johan tuned his violin, and they began the long dance through the whole cottage—into every corner, up and down every stairway, and then in a ring around the Christmas tree.

Esbjörn was tired, but he couldn't help being a bit curious, too. He sat down under the Christmas tree and felt all the Christmas packages carefully. He only wanted to know if they were soft or hard. He wanted one certain gift, and it was hard and not too big. What it was—this was known only to Esbjörn, and Johan, of course. For it was from Johan that he expected it.

The wood burning in the open fireplace are logs that Johan and Bäckström sawed at New Year's a year ago. Since then it was stacked in the woods, becoming fine and dry.

Almost everything in the picture came from the farm or was made there. The house and the workshop were rebuilt by Carl Larsson himself, the furnishings were made by him, and the walls were painted by him.

The food on the table came from Spadarvet. The rye in the bread was grown in the rye field, the splendid potatoes had been dug on the Kart hill, and the butter, cheese, and milk came from the cows on the farm.

Now almost everything lay at rest beneath the snow: the fall rye in the frozen hill and the clover and timothy grass in the pasture. Soon it would be spring again, and time for fishing and sowing and harrowing once more. In the meantime, there was wood to be cut, ice to be stored, and paintings to be finished.

CARL LARSSON was a painter and decorator who jolted the stagnating arts of book illustration and interior design at the turn of the century in Sweden. His youth was spent in poverty, but he managed to study at the Academy of Arts in Stockholm, where he won his first medal at age sixteen. Subsequent awards—three gold medals and a grant—enabled him to migrate to Paris in 1880, and from there to Grez, where he lived with a colony of Swedish open-air painters. In 1901 he moved from Stockholm to his house in Sundborn, where he remained the rest of his life.

In between his trips to France he began to work in watercolors, using fresh colors and diffused light, but when he finally settled in Sweden, he turned his attention to Japanese prints and Swedish folk art, and consequently, his style became more decorative and colorful.

In addition to painting, Larsson executed many murals with historical motifs, such as those on the walls of the National Museum in Sweden, without ceasing to devote himself to intimate watercolors of his family and home. It is these pictures that won him acclaim during his lifetime and, when collected in a book, changed the Swedish style of book illustration from being dull and lifeless to one of the finest European types of illustration.

As his family grew, Larsson began to see potential in the interior of his house, which was dark, as most were at that time. He painted the walls white and decorated doors, cabinets, and walls—whatever caught his eye at the moment—with flowers and folk designs. Soon the rooms were full of light and gay, bright colors. The selected pictures in his first book, A HOME, are watercolors of this cheerful home, portraits of his wife, Karin, and his children, which brought him well-deserved fame. They are full of Larsson's humor and reverence for all natural things—traits which endeared him to his own public and which made his paintings the classics they are.